Sedona on My Mind

Solo Piano Sheet Music
by Composer and Steinway Artist
Louis Landon

Louis Landon, formerly of New York and currently of Sedona, AZ, has dedicated his life to music. His passion is for peace. His career has taken him around the world playing a variety of styles with some of the most recognized names in the entertainment industry: classical music for Mikhail Baryshnikov on national and international tours, Latin music with "Pucho and his Latin Soul Brothers" on national and international tours, pop music with Rupert "Pina Colada Song" Holmes on television and national tours, rock & roll with John Hall, opening for "Little Feat" on national tours. For the past 26 years, through his production company, Landon Music Company, he has written and produced music for film, video and commercials, including three years of "best plays" and "bloopers" commercials for the National Basketball Association.

Not long ago, Landon realized that his music, the solo piano compositions that bring him so much joy and peace, could surely bring joy, and particularly peace, to millions around the world.

Louis Landon is currently working with three missions:
1. To create a more loving and peaceful world by writing, recording and performing, music from the heart.
2. To inspire people to live joyously and passionately.
3. To awaken and to assist people in healing themselves through music and mentoring.

He has released 16 CDs on the LCI record label, his latest entitled *Healing Hearts – Solo Piano*, was released on October 1, 2014 and contains music that was spontaneously composed during healing sessions.

Visit his website at louislandon.com for more information, CDs, sheet music, bookings, photos, videos, and tour dates.
For Healing Piano of Sedona information go to healingpianosedona.com
Louis Landon is available for Master Classes/Workshops in Improvisation
Create a Louis Landon Pandora station at pandora.com/louis-landon

Solo Piano Discography

2005 *unwind - solo piano*
2007 *Peace Revolution!*
2009 *Solo Piano for Peace*
2010 *Solo Piano for Love, Peace & Mermaids*
2011 *Peaceful Christmas - Solo Piano*
2012 *Peaceful Solo Piano from the Heart*
2013 *Ten Years - A Peaceful Solo Piano Retrospective*
2013 *Sedona on My Mind - Solo Piano*
2014 *Healing Piano of Sedona for massage, yoga and relaxation*
2014 *Healing Hearts - Solo Piano*

ISBN 978-0-9863062-7-3
©2015 Landon Creative, Inc.

Sedona on My Mind

Contents

Sedona on My Mind	1
Wide Open Spaces	7
Spring has Sprung	9
Leave the Past Behind	15
Beautiful Day	20
Silent Movie	23
The Chair	31
Sailor's Song	36
Sun on My Face	39
Play in Seven	44
Is This Good-bye?	50
Sunday Musings	53
Liberation	57

Sedona On My Mind

from the solo piano CD, *Sedona On My Mind*
Available from *www.louislandon.com*

LOUIS LANDON

Warm and contented (♩ = 126)

Copyright © 2013 Landon Creative, Inc. (BMI)
International Copyright Secured. All Rights Reserved.

Wide Open Spaces

from the solo piano CD, *Sedona On My Mind*
Available from *www.louislandon.com*

LOUIS LANDON

Copyright © 2013 Landon Creative, Inc. (BMI)
International Copyright Secured. All Rights Reserved.

Spring Has Sprung

from the solo piano CD, *Sedona On My Mind*
Available from www.louislandon.com

LOUIS LANDON

Copyright © 2013 Landon Creative, Inc. (BMI)
International Copyright Secured. All Rights Reserved.

Spring Has Sprung, Louis Landon

Leave the Past Behind

from the solo piano CD, *Sedona On My Mind*
Available from www.louislandon.com

LOUIS LANDON

Copyright © 2013 Landon Creative, Inc. (BMI)
International Copyright Secured. All Rights Reserved.

Leave the Past Behind, Louis Landon

Leave the Past Behind, Louis Landon

Beautiful Day

from the solo piano CD, *Sedona On My Mind*
Available from *www.louislandon.com*

LOUIS LANDON

Copyright © 2013 Landon Creative, Inc. (BMI)
International Copyright Secured. All Rights Reserved.

Silent Movie

from the solo piano CD, *Sedona On My Mind*
Available from www.louislandon.com

LOUIS LANDON

Copyright © 2013 Landon Creative, Inc. (BMI)
International Copyright Secured. All Rights Reserved.

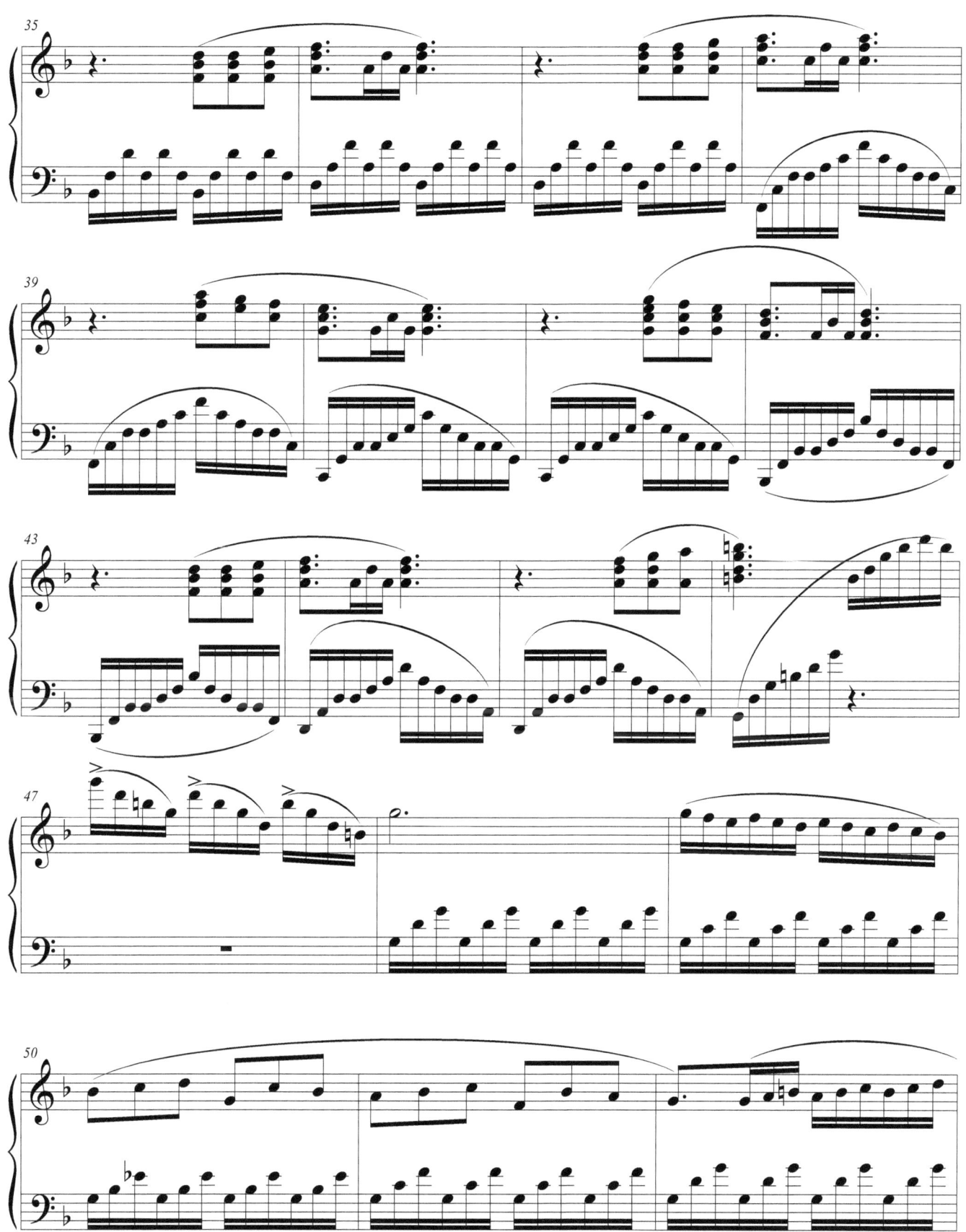

The Chair

from the solo piano CD, *Sedona On My Mind*
Available from www.louislandon.com

LOUIS LANDON

Relaxed, Peaceful (♩ = 63)

The Chair, Louis Landon

Sailor's Song

from the solo piano CD, *Sedona On My Mind*
Available from *www.louislandon.com*

LOUIS LANDON

Copyright © 2013 Landon Creative, Inc. (BMI)
International Copyright Secured. All Rights Reserved.

Sailor's Song, Louis Landon

Sun on My Face

from the solo piano CD, *Sedona on My Mind*
Available from *www.louislandon.com*

LOUIS LANDON

Sun on my Face, Louis Landon

Sun on my Face, Louis Landon

Play in Seven

from the solo piano CD, *Sedona on My Mind*
Available from *www.louislandon.com*

LOUIS LANDON

Play in Seven, Louis Landon

Play in Seven, Louis Landon

Is This Good-bye?

from the solo piano CD, *Sedona on My Mind*
Available from www.louislandon.com

LOUIS LANDON

Copyright © 2013 Landon Creative, Inc. (BMI)
International Copyright Secured. All Rights Reserved.

Is this Good-Bye? Louis Landon

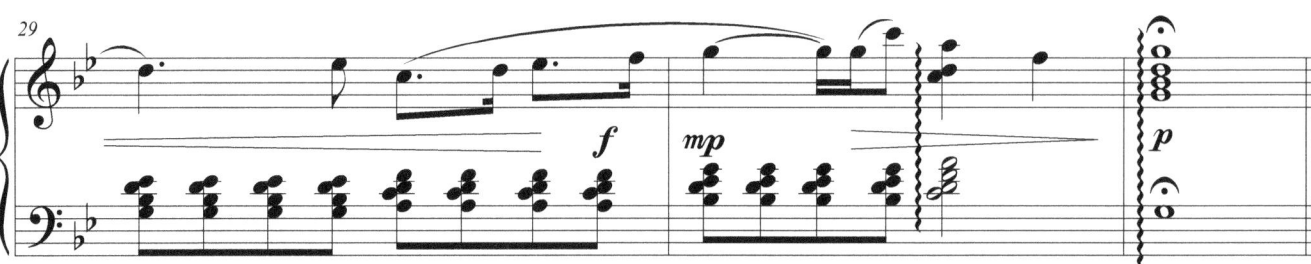

Sunday Musings

from the solo piano CD, *Sedona on My Mind*
Available from *www.louislandon.com*

LOUIS LANDON

Liberation

from the solo piano CD, *Sedona on My Mind*
Available from www.louislandon.com

LOUIS LANDON

Copyright © 2013 Landon Creative, Inc. (BMI)
International Copyright Secured. All Rights Reserved.

Liberation, Louis Landon

ISBN 978-0-9863062-7-3

www.ingramcontent.com/pod-product-compliance
Lightning Source LLC
Chambersburg PA
CBHW041538220426
43663CB00002B/70